MW00902599

This music business book looks to guide an individual pursuing music as a career with direction. We will look at various artists, statistics, and reports to inform you. All information has been thoroughly researched and observed within the industry.

First paperback edition June 2019

Book designed by Darrius Ford, Founder of Pryme Art Agency

Biography written by Nate Spurlin, Founder of OLDMLK

ISBN: 978-0-359-37317-8

www.guidedbyobas.com

This book is dedicated to my family both related and non-related. Yes, some artists are a part of this.

Love ya a ton!

Table of Contents

Introduction

Welcome to *Shifting Your Music into a Career: A Guide for Independent Artists to be Full Time Artists*! This is something that is going to change your views on the music industry as whole. Each volume is going to give you a taste of what goes on in my mind when dealing with the indie-stry. If you are not familiar with the term indie-stry, it is a term I like to use to describe the market for emerging artists. In this market, I deal with artists who lack the resources such as knowledge or money to turn their music into a career. The goal of these books is for artists to understand the music industry clearer and utilize my guidance to find direction with their music. As a result, artists should start seeing increase in streams, sales, and more importantly knowledge of the music industry.

In this volume, we observe and understand cases studies involving artists such as Travis Scott, De La Soul, Daft Punk, Jay Rock, and even Frank Ocean. We also look at research from other music business writers and personal observations I have seen in the indie-stry. We are focusing on important topics like brand image, social media, streaming platforms, and record deals that are crucial things to mention when you are in the music industry. You will also see some of the projects I have consulted on as they have seen the success of my guidance. I hope that you will see it too. So, enough of me, doing what they call "Introductions", and let us dive into the first volume.

Mirror, Mirror of an Artist

Professor DefBeat is here to teach us! Who?! You may say! Professor DefBeat is the Hip-Hop icon from **De La Soul's** video, "Me, Myself, and I". I had to bring him to life in our first chapter to talk about image and how it hurts or elevates artists! So, take out those notebooks and jot down some notes because I, Obas, am done talking and will allow the legend to talk!

Professor DefBeat: Image is the most important thing in the music game! It can either hurt you or elevate you! Why is that?

Class: We don't know! We just started rapping, and it seemed fun! Our friends encouraged us to do it!

Professor DefBeat: It's a good thing that you don't know! Image is important because it helps the audience distinguish an artist from another artist. Today, it is hard to distinguish artists when we all have the same fashion style or same rhyme scheme! Back in my days, De la Soul was known for being the weirdos! Anyone know why?

Class: Cuz they were different!

Professor DefBeat: Exactly! From clothes to music, they were different and true to themselves. They produced songs such as, "Me, Myself, and I" and "Buddy", which defined their distinct sound. Now a days, you guys want to run around talking about Dracos, henny bottles, and strip clubs. Really guys?! The crazy part about it is that you are not about that life. Your fans know who you are.

Class: Wow!

Professor DefBeat: I know. However, today, we solve that issue! Here's my advice. Start rapping or singing about things involving around your life and passion! You can grab more listeners and distinguish your brand from others! By doing this, you are more marketable. This is what made De la Soul different from other hip-hop groups like Tribe Called Quest. I believe each one of you have the capability to do the same. Just do it!

Class: Thanks Professor DefBeat!

Professor DefBeat: Anytime! Until next time! See ya soon and be different!

A ton of people will call me corny for this skit, but I don't care. The main thing I'm driving into your damn brains is the importance of brand image. With a different and attractable brand image, you can take your music to new heights. It really just starts with you going into the mirror, looking at your story and music, and telling it in ways people have never seen before. I hope I gave you the foundation as this idea will reappear in the upcoming chapters of this book.

The Performance Effect

I'm introducing a new term in the music industry called **The Performance Effect** because no one else has done it. The Performance Effect is the results an artist experience after an extraordinary performance. It can be a purchase of a merchandise, an increase in streams, or more fans in future shows. If you had to put it in some equation, because I love math and I'm a nerd, it would be this

+ Performance = +Revenue Streams and Fan Base

A good performance has a direct relationship with revenue streams and fan base. The thing that kind of stays constant here is the artists. **Travis Scott** is a perfect example of using this Performance Effect. He performed "Goosebumps" 15 times in Oklahoma City back in 2016, which was ground breaking. After the performance, the plays on that individual song increased by about 10%, according to Billboard magazine. If it wasn't for his performance, do you honestly think his plays would have increased by that much or people would be excited for his future releases like *AstroWorld?* Let's apply this concept to the indie-stry then.

Independent artists don't realize the significance of their performances. You guys must bring the energy every time you perform despite crowd size. There can be 1 or 100 people watching you perform, but all you need is that one influencer who can say, "That kid's performance is amazing. I want to go to another show." That individual is going to tell another person and another person. Eventually, people will know you and you don't know them. That is when the numbers start to increase in fan base and revenue streams. You know what I call that… A LEVEL UP! If you don't know how to perform well, then continue to read this book because we will talk about how you can perform well to achieve this "**Performance Effect**".

The performance effect is a great thing if done right. By going all out on your performances, you have a chance to do a lot for yourself. Gain new fans, make money, or increase streams are the things that come after a great performance. However, choose not to perform well by being cheap or not paying for performances (not talking about dumb pay 2 play performances), watch how you jeopardize your career as one of my former mentors, **Blackout The Rebel,** always states. The choice is all yours, so make the right one.

Moving Through Streaming Platforms

The number one thing that is on every artist's mind is <u>Streaming</u>. Every artist wants to have their music streaming on every platform to show they are an artist. However, artists don't have a single clue on how to navigate through **Spotify, Apple Music, and Tidal**. So, this part of the book is going to give you brief descriptions of each major streaming service and ways you can utilize these platforms to increase your value as an artist.

Spotify is the number #1 globally used streaming platform in the world. I would say Spotify's main target is college students in my opinion. With $4.99, students can watch shows on Showtime and Hulu while streaming unlimited music. However, the artist payout is the lowest out of the three platforms. In 2018, Spotify paid an emerging artist $0.003 per stream. That isn't S***! A platform that is the #1 globally used isn't paying artists the most money? Interesting right?! So, here are ways, you, the artist can navigate through this platform:

<u>Spotify Pointers:</u>

- Make Sure **No One** has the same name as you. See this way too often!!
  - o If someone does, do two things
    - Contact Spotify to make modifications
    - Change something about your name. Drop a vowel or just completely change it
- Need to Link Twitter, Instagram, and Facebook to Spotify

- You can increase followers on other social media platforms as people listen to your music.
- Look great on Spotify---- Get a nice profile pic
  - This picture must give listeners a sense of your aesthetic and brand.
- Demand people to Follow Your Artist Page on Spotify ***
  - People get notifications (email and on Spotify) when you release new music, and it appears on their New Music section
    - Music is automatically placed on New Release and Discover Weekly Playlist on personalized user account as a result of following the artists.
- Sell Merch through Spotify
  - Research MerchBar.
    - With this platform, you can sell merch on your Spotify account.
- Social Sharing
  - Instagram is powerful here for you can do two things.
    - Put song cover art in story
    - Add the song as background music. (check with distribution company)
  - Twitter: Gives 30 second snippet of the song
  - Facebook: not much to say here besides attach the link to post
- Make Presave(s) available for audience.
  - When you make Presave(s) available, users get notifications that the song is available once it drops via email.
- Build music catalogue ***********IMPORTANT**

- o Want to maintain monthly listeners because these can drop and rise every month
  - ▪ Drop music constantly, but not excessively (will talk soon about this)
  - ▪ Features: This builds up your "Artist Appears On" section.
  - ▪ If you do the first two points well, this builds the Spotify Radio for an artist.
- Encourage people to download and save songs
- Playlists
  - o Encourage people to add songs to their personalized playlists
  - o Look for Spotify editorial playlists and/or Spotify curators
- Sign up for Spotify for Artists
  - o Read Analytics
    - ▪ Look at Trending songs--- want to promote these songs and create music videos to these trending songs (at times)
    - ▪ Locations- look to organize tours and performances around areas
    - ▪ Look at Gender- highly encourage that your girl to boy listeners ratio is high to girls. Girls are great influencers when it comes to the music industry.
- Touring/ Concerts:
  - o Every time you have a performance, it should show up on Spotify. Link it with Song Kick! It should take about 24 hours to appear on Spotify profile. Incorporate artists who will perform with you, so it appears on their profile.

Apple Music is the 2nd streaming service that is important to mention. It pays artists about $0.008 per stream, and it's the second globally used music streaming platform out of the three mentioned above. For some reason, a ton of Apple music listeners are from the United States. This is a crucial point to mention, for a ton of United States artists should be gearing their marketing campaign to this geographic segment. In addition, you can't really fake your streams here as well lol. (Too soon for that haha) Back to the course! Here are your pointers on how to move through this platform:

Apple Music Pointers

- Apple Music Connect:
    - Build a connection with your fans. Encourage followers on Apple Music
- Treat Apple Music as if it was social media. Can only be done if you completed Pointer 1. DO this and you will be good.
    - Post links to music and encourage engagement.
- Similar to Spotify:
    - Encourage playlists
    - Build music catalogue
- Artist Radio
    - Very easy here compared to Spotify, but different where Apple Music will randomize tracks on these radios. Kind of like Soundcloud.
        - However, artists still need features and a good amount of music.
- Encourage people to like your tracks (engagement)******
    - When you introduce it to someone unfamiliar, they are more likely to click the likable ones.
- Sign Up for Apple Music for Artists
    - Pay Attention to the Trends Section

- Specifically, the Change column. You want to promote the tracks that have high percentage of change.
  - Pay Attention to Location
    - You want to see where your listeners are tuning into your music
    - Possibly organizing TOUR??? IDK
- Presales and Purchases via ITUNES
  - It's okay that people don't buy albums these days. The trend shows it. However, it's a huge problem if you don't make this available for people to purchase. Make this available! You never know who may purchase it for the support. In addition, THIS IS A REVENUE GENERATOR. Don't be a goofball and disregard this.

Our final streaming platform is none other than Sean Carter's platform, **Tidal**. Tidal is the highest paying streaming platform out of the three listed above. It pays artists a whole penny per stream. That's a lot right there lol! The app offers Master Quality Authenticated Technology. This means it delivers that rich quality music. {big words for no reason here} Finally, it offers listeners various packages to become subscribers to it. The downfall of Tidal is the UX design. There is really no customer experience with the product where the customer can interact with the app on a daily base and stay fully engaged with the app. This is kind of the reason why it is the lowest of the three platforms for subscribers. It still is a developing app, but I do have some pointers that will help you navigate through it.

Tidal Pointers

1. Switch Subscribers to Tidal

a. This is tough since you are battling with Spotify and Apple Music. You don't want to force your listeners to convert.
   i. Incentivize that you can make more money here
2. Look at Tidal Rising
   a. This program is still developing, but it could be a strength for Tidal in the future as it helps artists grow
3. If you know your Tidal supporters, identify them and encourage them to stream a ton.

There are many other streaming platforms for you. Funny enough, Xbox Live pays very well. I want to say close to 2 pennies haha. However, if you think streaming is going to pay your bills, you better stick to flipping burgers at McDonalds because you are not making any money with streams. These pointers give you the tools you need to really make the most money out of your streams. Think of streams as your bonus checks! It just adds to your other revenue streams. If you follow these pointers, you can easily make streaming your best friend instead of something you need to tackle.

The Crowd Goes "Fund"!

It has always been between **Tribe Called Quest** and **De La Soul** for me. Unfortunately, De La Soul was viewed as the lesser of the two. They are still a dope group to learn from especially if we are talking about the indie-stry. This group had legit no money to get a campaign going for their album, *And the Anonymous Nobody*. The label didn't give them money, the publishing didn't give them money, not even their distribution. So, who gave them the money for the album?! The FANS! In this chapter, we are going to talk about the importance of something that business people love to talk about as a revenue generator, CROWDFUNDING, a thing artist need to start thinking about! You will see in this chapter the benefit of this and what are the results that come when using crowdfunding. Let's go.

As stated before, De La Soul didn't have the financial backing of a label to generate money for their album. In 2016, they decided to start a campaign on Kickstarter to raise money for their album. The campaign goal was to raise $200k-$300k. The campaign ended up making double the amount because De La Soul fans appreciated the group and their craft. The fans wanted to see the Hip-Hop legend succeed. In addition, the group got a Grammy nomination for the album. That is such a great story right there. Your fans being able to fund for your career because they support your music and your dream. Amazing! How can we apply this lesson to the indie-stry?!

For emerging artists, I highly suggest you start a campaign for any of your music especially come touring time. It will reduce your out of pocket expense and allow you to put more effort into your music. However, to start a campaign, you need to turn your fans and followers into believers. Believers will invest their money into your dream. This only comes when your image is developed and genuine. So, if you have these qualities, why wouldn't you run a campaign?!

Money is always a problem, but if you can reduce this with the help of your believers, why not make crowdfunding an option. You will reduce a major amount of your expenses. You can generate a greater profit margin by doing this. You may not want to go with this option because you may have this weird stereotype that crowdfunding is begging people for money lol. No, it is not begging, but asking. You are asking for help to accomplish your dreams. Don't be stubborn my friend. Utilize this option when needed. You won't go wrong with this. All the love.

Mama, Can I be a Frank Ocean?!

If you are a self-releasing artist and you ask your mother the question, "Can I be a Frank Ocean?", she should honestly look at you differently. In this day of age, you do not want to be a **Frank Ocean**! I love the guy, but it has to stop here. What do I mean?! Frank Ocean hasn't released an album or mixtape since *Blonde*, which came out in 2016. Brother, I'm sorry, but it is 2019. You can't even give me an EP! Sorry, but not! If Frank Ocean was just starting today, I don't think he would be as big as he is. Today, we are going to talk about why Frank Ocean is a special breed and why you, the self-releasing artist, cannot and should not attempt to follow Frank Oceans' steps. This will be tough to tackle, but we are going to do it because it needs to be said.

Frank Ocean might be one of this generation's best alternative R&B artist I've seen. His albums really put one in a very introspective mood, where we are really thinking about ourselves. He has been able to release music easily until 2016 where he finessed Universal Music Group and released *Blonde* under his own label. Way to go bruh, but that was then, this is now. It's 2019, and Frank Ocean has teased us multiple times of new music and still no project. He mentioned new music on his IG last year in November, but still hasn't came out with a project. The reason why people still stream his music is that they love his voice and have bonded with his projects. There's a true connection there. I personally can't let go of *Channel Orange* and *Nostalgia/Ultra*, but this is about bashing Frank Ocean haha. If Frank Ocean was an emerging artist, could he still drop a project every 3 or more years?! Overall, Frank Ocean can do this now since he got the fans, but I don't think emerging artists can do this especially now.

Artists, you have to put out music at a consistent rate based on the fans and the market. Why? Some of you don't have that true hard core fanbase like Frank Ocean when you can drop an EP or an LP, and then go ghost for 3 years or more for another album. In addition, your monthly listeners on Spotify will go down if the music you have out doesn't have playback value. Even if you don't want to put out another album immediately after the first one, you should be constantly promoting the music you have out now as creatively as possible. Remixing some of your songs are definitely a way of doing it. Your old fans will demand you to put out new music, however, you will be gaining new fans who never heard your music if you creatively promote it. In a very simple point: balance between releases and have a true understanding of what state your market is. Do your fans need music, or can they wait?! You can only tell this based on the demand of your fans and the state of the market.

Frank Ocean, again, will always be a legend, but if he did this nonsense as a self-releasing artist with no fans, his career would go down the toilet. I don't care how good his music is, the listeners are what keep your career running. It is your job as an artist to deliver music at a constant rate. The constant rate is not dropping every 3 years and expecting your fans will stay with you. It is a rate that satisfies your fans while strategically putting out music.

So, the lesson to take away is that you can be a Frank Ocean, just make sure you have that core fanbase who can wait on your next project and you know the demand. Peace and keep it nostalgia and ultra.

Artist Spotlight: Ursa Major

I can never call this individual by his first name because I met him as an artist first. This individual is one of my favorite emerging artists in the indie-stry from Long Island. This individual is **Ursa Major**. I met Ursa Major at SXSW with **Nikmoody,** an artist I consulted with as well. Since I met this man, Ursa Major opened for **Wyclef Jean** and **Kota The Friend**. In addition, this man has traveled everywhere in the United States and has collected passport stamps in Haiti and Paris. What amazes me about Ursa Major is not only his music, but his versatility as an entrepreneur. This man makes music, creates showcases for artists at Amityville Hall, and manages a label called, Label Noir. I can never be disappointed with the moves this man makes because he is always plotting, finessing, and elevating.

I respect the man, for he is always learning, teaching, and chilling. You should give **Ursa Major** a follow-on Spotify and see his movements on social media. Connect with Ursa Major. You won't be disappointed. Thanks, my man. Always love. Now back to these short chapters.

Becoming an Artist:
The Artist Prelude (Part 1)

Friend: Bruh, I'm about to be an artist. I got a studio, a mixing software, and some mics.

Me: Seriously! (Laughing to myself)

Friend: Yeah, I just don't know what to do after that.

In the mini scenario above, my friend is simply trying to become an artist. He has some of the tools to get it done, but he doesn't know where to go from there. My friend is going through the first stage of becoming an artist I like to call, **The Artist Prelude**. In this stage, the artist is trying to find their sound that represents their brand through recording, lyricism and beat production. In this chapter, we are going to talk about the first stage and how does one move step by step through it. If the artist can get through this process, his or her track will be ready to distribute hopefully.

The Artist Prelude is the steps an artist must take before making their music available for distribution. This stage gives an artist a ton of creative room to make music. However, if you don't have money to start, you might as well stop right there because you will fully see that getting through the Artist Prelude requires $$$$$. Let us work through the process.

1. Beat Selection: Your job is to find beats that represents your brand and image. You can get it from producers, sample (highly difficult to attain clearance), or YouTube beat types.

Just make sure where you are getting the beat that it is exclusive and unique.

2. **Written Composition:** This is where we get the storytelling of the artist. You need inspiration here in this stage. Put yourself in a creative space to write. You need to be extremely genuine in your words, for what you say is a direct reflection of your brand. Be creative with your words, use references, double meaning, metaphors, other poetic techniques to create that brand message. If you can't do this, get yourself a songwriter.

*Note: Some people like to write, and then find the beat. I always find this way more effective in my opinion.

3. **Budgeting:** See how much money you have for studio time, mix and mastering, marketing, and more. You want to create your budget based on affordability. If you can't afford most of the stuff, reduce the cost and focus on the main objectives or just get a more hours at your job.
   a. Example: I am an artist and my starting budget is $300 for a single. Maybe $150 for recording studios, $100 for promotion, and $50 for cover art. The assumption in this case is that you know people who can give you deals or do it for free and I release it on Audiomack and Soundcloud.

Note: Free doesn't always equate to best quality

4. **Recording:** Here's where a ton of you artists stop because you don't have the money for studio time. Studio time can range from $25 an hour to $60 an hour or even more. You will not be able to get all the work you need done in the studio. In

addition, some studios will give you the space without the engineer, so you may have to bring your own or pay for the inhouse engineer which can cost again.

    a. To reduce cost, build an inhouse studio or go to a friend's house. Build the skeleton of the track! When you go to the studio, all you need to do is just mix and master. I've seen this work with Syracuse artist, **Seth Dollar**, and how he constructed ***"Refs Since Thursday",*** which consisted of 3 songs.

    b. Another way to reduce cost is to find an engineer that can do it for free. Ask and shoot your shot.

5. Mix and Mastering: These are two different things. Mixing is putting all your edits on vocals and instrumentals to form this one stereo audio file. Mastering is putting the final touches on the pieces to really get it right. You can't avoid this step even if you try because it won't sound pleasing.

6. Cover Art: This is the final process of **The Artist Prelude**. Be as creative as you want. Just two things. Just don't make it look ugly and get a cover art that makes sense or sparks curiosity. The average price is $35. This isn't that bad to be honest.

If you can complete these 6 steps, you are setting yourself up for the next stage of becoming an artist, **The Distribution**. The only way you can move is to follow these steps listed above. We will be discussing the 2nd step to becoming an artist in the next book, but this should have given you a starting point.

Becoming an Artist Diagram

The Artist Prelude

The Distribution

The Rollout

The Project

The Artist Interlude

Where Those Playlists At?!

Alex: Everyone from artists to the label are searching for this one thing. It is not gold.

Me: What is a Playlist?!

Alex: Correct for $500.

If only Alex asked me this question on Jeopardy, I would be the happiest person because I would walk away with $500 to pay my bills lol. To bring it back to reality though, it is true what Alex states. Labels and artists are constantly looking for playlists. Why?! Playlists allow artists to be discovered while boosting their streams. Playlists create a certain theme or mood for their audience without the audience having the slightest idea of the tracks. You will see a specific label, publishing company, or media outlet with their playlist because they are trying to promote the artists on their roster while creating a mood for the audience. However, it is not easy for one to be placed on these playlists or easy to find one. This chapter is going to talk about how artists' songs can be placed in these playlists. From a grand scheme, it seems easy, but it is tough! Trust me, we will get through this.

The first step in acquiring a playlist placement is always figuring out what genre, lifestyle, or mood the song is. Why?! Playlists give an unknown listener an idea what kind of tracks they are getting themselves into. They are introduced to the tracks by the title and the description of the playlists. Ex: If I am an artist and I am rapping about my latest purchase of Gucci, playlists that will kind of define that track are: hip-hop, rap, or fashion if those elements are incorporated in the track. As an independent artist, you must identify what mood and genre your song fits in. This is such a pivotal point in pitching to these playlists. If you or your team cannot do this, you lost the battle to obtain a playlist before sending it out.

Once you identified the theme/genre/mood of the song(s), you can start sending these to people who curate playlists. But Obas, I don't know where I can pitch it to or how to get them?! Well, you can start by sending it to **Spotify for Artists, Indiemono,** or local media outlets like Lyrical Lemonade that curate playlists for their audience. In addition, you can tell your friends to add your song to their playlist. These are free and simple to do. There's no guaranteeing that your music will make these playlists, but it's worth a try. If you want a guarantee placement, then you must pay. This brings us to our second route to the playlists.

Artists want their music guaranteed on playlists. They want to start building those looks. They want the industry to say, "That artist is taking off!" Well artists, there are multiple platforms such as **Spotify Plugger**, **Sound Plate**, **Playlist Pushers** who insert your song(s) to many different playlists. You only need the minimum budget of $150 to get your song(s) placed for these platforms. With that minimum budget, you can put a song for as long as you want. As a result, you will see your streams go pass 1,000, but that doesn't equate to having 1000 fans now or making you a better artist… C'mon now… Do better lol!

Playlists are cute! They show that you are trending or my favorite word, popping. There's a possibility you could be the next big thing. I just have a couple of questions for you. What are streams if you don't have fans?! What are streams if you can't sell out shows?! More importantly, what are streams if you don't have no money?! Playlists are the thing that will get you exposure, but they are not going to feed your family and sustain your career. It is good to know the significance of them and how to enter into them, but you shouldn't be depending on them to make or break your career. Get the exposure from playlists. Really consider this question: Will the playlist be the X factor between you and your career?! You can figure it out if this is important because I did my part. Peace.

The Music Rubric

Let's have a laugh first! Do you recall the show, American Idol?! It used to come on ABC I believe. When I was younger, I recall a moment when Randy Jackson told this guy wearing a flamingo suit to just get off the stage. I didn't understand it back then, but now I do. His delivery was trash! My dad and I were dying in tears. Artists love to present people with new music and don't know what people are looking for. How does an artist avoid this embarrassing moment like the flamingo guy?! Using **The Music Rubric**, one can avoid this I say. We are going to try to define a generic one in this chapter for our purposes to see where your music fits. Let's Go!

The Music Rubric is **NOT** a rubric that you can find online, but most people use these categories to critique music. These are not rules, but things people look for to give their honest opinion on a track. Below, you will find the categories that people may use to critique music. You should also use this to critique your own music.

1. Lyricism: **What is your story/message?** This is where the listeners find the artist's purpose. Things that fall in this category: Double meanings, Word Choice, and Rhyming scheme.
2. Delivery: **How do you present this story/message?** This is where the people can feel the story/message. Things that fall in this category: Voice, Language, Pace
3. Creativity/ Originality: **Can you craft a song using your own ideas or ideas of others before you that sparks interest?** Music critics study music. If they can identify that a song is a direct replication of another song, you are in boiling waters. Delivery and Lyricism play a major role when trying to accomplish successfully the creativity and originality category.

Things that can fall here are sampling, referencing, and usage of autotune.

4. Production: This is very similar to the Creativity/ Originality category. However, the question that you should ask, **"Without the lyrics, does the instrumental bump?"** People are looking for beats that are pleasant to the ear. Things that fall in this category: Live Instruments and 808.

5. Mixing and Mastering: **"What are you adding to the song to give it an extra boost?"** This is where a great audio engineer is needed. Things that fall in this category: Sound effects, Faders, and EQ.

6. Marketing: **"How are you, the artist, delivering your music to your listeners?"** This is where I believe a lot of artists struggle and lose their career. Artists are not focused on the business aspect of the music industry smh. As a result, their brand takes a major toll. A couple of things that fall into this category: Lyricism (specifically hooks or catchy phrases), Fashion, Audience, Resources, Presence. Very Important you understand this category.

7. Potential: One simple question answer this, **"Can you and your song produce a HIT?"** If you can do everything right from categories 1 to 6, I don't see why you can't make a Hit.

This is an intensive rubric. With constant studying, you will know what **The Music Rubric** is in the back of your mind. Understanding this rubric will be key for any independent artist that submits their track to any media outlet, any artist showcase, or any friend. It will help you produce a better track overall once you understand this. As a result, your audience should expand because the music is promoting for you now. Make a note of this chapter and the next, because I guarantee you, this will reappear every time you are thinking about your music career.

The Performance Rubric

A couple of years ago, like 2006 I want to say, **Daft Punk** had one of their greatest performances at Coachella. The stage was intense. The crowd was engaged. The experience was memorable. Since Daft Punk was able to put on a show, Daft Punk was able to turn their 1 ½ hour set to something worth watching for years and years again. You can say, "They mastered **The Performance Effect**." (Love using my own terms) True, but they also understood what was required for them to perform well. That is what we are going to talk about here in this chapter, **The Performance Rubric**, is what we are going to call these requirements.

A few months ago, I was asked to judge a performance. An artist came to me and asked me why he didn't place. I told him straight up there was no artist/crowd engagement, and his clothes didn't match his music aesthetics. He wanted to know how I judge performances. This is **NOT** a standard rubric or a set of rules, but it gives you a sense what people look for at shows or showcases. Some topics may overlap with our Music Rubric, so here we go.

1. Stage Presence: **"*How do you utilize the stage or space to enhance your performance*"?!**
    o This is very simple. Utilize what space you have effectively to create an experiential moment where the audience can remember you and your setting. Add lights or visual background to enhance stage presence. These are examples.
2. Artist/Crowd Engagement: **"*How are you interacting with the crowd*"?**
    o This category humbles you down to where you are a human. You should try to have convos with the audience, do some call and respond tracks, or bring another artist on your set. These are examples. The goal is that you

want to build a bond with your fans while having fun. You can only do it by engaging with them.

3. Production: **"*Are you rapping/singing or is your mp3 doing it for you*"?!**
    - This part is where some of you lose the audience when you are performing. They can't hear what you are saying because you let the production dominate your vocals. You need to lower instrumentals on tracks or have a performance track, so we can hear the lyricism and delivery. Not saying you ditch the mp3 completely because long sets are tiring, and you need those to support, but the whole set? Nah fam! Next haha.
    - If the set ranges between 10-15 minutes, you should be able to do ONLY instrumentals assuming you engage with the audience.

4. Fashion: **" *What in the world are you wearing?*"**
    - Understand how you dress and how does your apparel match your music and brand. Example: I don't expect a hipster to wear Timberlands like WTF, that don't match. Dress smart.

5. Marketability: Again, this category, **"*How does an artist deliver their content to the crowd?*"**
    - This category is complicated. You are delivering your music, your performance, and your brand to your fans. You want to make sure you have things prepared for people to notice it. Flyer, stickers, and merch are things you should have at your show. This will increase your brand presence while delivering your music to them.

6. Creativity/Originality: **"When a thing(s) goes wrong, can you figure out a way to keep the performance alive?"**
    - This can occur when the audience is not engaged, sound messes up, or the promoter does a terrible job organizing the event! You need to figure out how to bring things in order. Example: A Capella or Impromptu works here.

7. Potential: One simple question answer this, "**Can you and your Performance influence others to book you or have you at their show?**" Answer to this can be found in **"The Performance Effect"** chapter.

The only way to have a good performance is to practice your set. Practice will get you ready for the stage and the audience. In addition, reduce problem come game day. By doing this constantly, you can do a 10, 20, and 45 minutes slot easily. Just practice your craft and follow this rubric. Once you do this, you are able to guide people to your music where you will see growth everywhere. Again that, **The Performance Effect**, we love it haha!

Snap Me, Then I'm Gone

Ah, everyone's favorite platform, SNAPCHAT! The app that deletes your stories within 24hours, so no one can see your drunk, f***** up nights. The glory of a dying app is so great! Hold up….. did I just say dying?! I did, and it's an app I constantly recommend artists and brands to not promote. By the end of this chapter, you will see my reasons to avoid the app and what I recommend instead of Snapchat.

As reported in Snapchat's 2017 10K, Snapchat generated $824,949 in revenue and a total of costs and expenses of $4,310,525. Let that resonate with you for a second. The company generated more costs and expenses in the 2017 year than revenue not including interest expenses. S***! In addition, the company's expenses have almost doubled since 2015. That's insane to me! So, let me sum all this up in one sentence for you to understand. **The company is not making any money or profit!** I'm sorry, but it is true. This company may either be bought out or just go out of business. They can't generate profit!! So, why waste your time on promoting an app that may financially go out of business?! That's one you may have not known. The second one is a simple observation and you should be able to see this.

I don't know if you noticed, but Instagram has been on a roll with its updates especially with the introduction of the IG stories. You have the option to send those private drunk, crazy videos to close friends and family. This is very similar to Snapchat. As a result of these updates, Instagram has increased their daily users tremendously since the introduction of this feature. Don't believe me! Check what I'm about to say. Reported by CNBC in 2018, Instagram accumulated 400 million daily users after introducing the IG stories in 2016. Snapchat has been around since 2014 and hasn't even touched those numbers. It took Instagram less than a year and a half to surpass Snapchat's daily users. How can Snapchat compete with Instagram?! They can't haha. If the daily users continue to increase for Instagram, we are going to see users from Snapchat move to Instagram I believe. However, artists, you are still going to promote Snapchat, right?! Ya weirdos lol.

To wrap this up, I've provided you two legit points on why Snapchat is not an app you should be promoting. They don't make money, and Instagram is blowing them out the waters. As an artist or a brand, you don't want to invest your promotional efforts on a platform that is on the brink of being extinct. Move your efforts to other meaningful social media platforms like Facebook, Twitter, or Instagram to increase your brand awareness. Peace.

The 1x, 2x, 3x, etc. Technique

Did you ever ask yourself why **Drake's** "God's Plan" streams are incredibly high?! Well, you can thank this new technique, "**The single, double, triple, etc. technique**", I am introducing to the industry. The single, double, triple, etc. technique is probably the most confusing technique in the industry, however it is probably the most effective technique that will carry your streams over and over again while the numbers increase. You will see a song or even an album be released multiple times in different ways, but the streams just keep adding up despite the amount of times it has been released. It doesn't make sense now, but I think its crucial for us to put it into context using an artist I thought I would never use.... **Jay Rock** and his album, ***Redemption***, specifically his hit single, "King's Dead". La di da di let's get it on.

Before I can put Jay Rock into context with the technique, I think it is pivotal that I define it and its significance. **The single, double, triple, etc. technique** is the amount of times an artist releases a single or album to their audience. It doesn't matter how many times the artist releases the track if it's dope and released in many different ways, then people will stream it. The significance of this technique is that an artist is adding streams every time it's released. You don't necessarily need a playlist if you use this technique haha. Crazy right! It doesn't make sense now, but as we work through the Jay Rock example it will make sense.

So now comes the hard part haha... explaining the technique! Shoot! Throughout the explanation, we will use "King's Dead" and another hypothetical situation to explain the technique. Please stay with me here haha because it will be confusing.

- Single (1x) Release: This is extremely straightforward. As an artist, you just release the single once and call it a day. If you feature an artist, it will appear on their artist profile on Spotify, but still come up as one release.
    - Example: TDE releases "King's Dead" as a single, and you went crazy. BOOM!
- Double (2x) Release: This is about to get complicated for there is two ways to finesse this haha. The goal for the double release is that you are trying to get users to stream the song at double the rate or add streams to the first release of the song.
    - Example 1: Let's say **Eddie Hayes**, *CEO of Underscore LLC*, and I came up with a single and both of us were under Underscore LLC. What we could do is release it both on our individual artist profile page. The streams will run 2x the rate since fans of both Eddie and I will stream the song. The common denominator is that we release under the same company name
        - Simple formula here: 2x (Artist Release) = total streams
    - Example 2: TDE releases "King's Dead" as a single and hits 800,000 streams. Now, what they do is release it as a compilation, ***Black Panther.*** What happened with the stream of "King's Dead"?! It didn't start from 0. Nope, it started from that 800,000 like I mentioned and added the new release streams.
        - Formula: 800,000+ whatever streams of 2nd release=total release
- Triple (3x) Release: If you understand the second one clearly, then this triple release technique should make sense now.
    - Example 1: Let's stick with the Eddie and I example. We released the single which hit 400,000 on my platform and 200,000 on his platform. For a total of 600,000 streams. Why not?! Let's do an album!

- New formula: 400,000+ 200,000+ whatever the streams on album is= total streams of single
  - Example 2: Let's start from scratch and incorporate the whole *Underscore LLC* group excluding me out of it because I don't have bars. Let's get **Joshua Brooks** and **Dante Stewart,** who are also founders of the company. Three artists on a single... Hm 3x the streams. Yup, rock it.
    - Formula: 3x (Artists Releases) = Total Streams
  - Example 3: Back to "King's Dead"! TDE released it as single, incorporated it in *Black Panther* album. Now, Top Dawg decides to hit up Jay Rock and incorporate it in his album, *Redemption*.
    - Formula: Single Release+ compilation+ album= total streams

Amazing right! I can keep going on and on about the many different release techniques. That is why I incorporated the etc. part. The basis of this technique is if you release or deliver your music multiple times to your listeners uniquely, the listeners will continue to stream your music weirdly enough. If you can tell I love formulas, so I am going to give you one that brings everything together haha.

Let R represent the amount of times you release your music.

$$R_1 + R_2 + R_3 + \ldots\ldots\ldots\ldots\ldots + R_n = \text{Total streams of song/album}$$

This technique is assuming that you are under the same company as an individual, you have a good relationship with artists and fans, and more importantly, the music is attractive and has playback value. Your brand will take a major toll if you use the technique and force it down people's throat. So, before trying this technique, release it once see what the market thinks. If the fans mess with it, then continue to present it in many creative ways. Peace.

Can we get a Deal?!

The thing that almost every artist wants to do is have a chance to sit down with an executive from one of the three major labels: **Universal Music Group, Sony Entertainment**, or **Warner Bros**. Artists want this so bad since the label is a major resource for artists to have a career. I just don't know how long the label is going to hold you and your music until you are drained out, but that's a different story. More importantly, the goal for this final chapter is to explain why you, an artist, let's say 5K followers on IG may not have the same opportunity as someone with 10K. (Assuming the 10K is genuine) This will give you some insight, but also motivate you to work harder to get that meeting.

Every week, the label, specifically the A&R department, is working steadily finding the newest artists to sign. They have their ears to the street, eyes on the computer, and hands on everything around them involving the music scene. The A&R department is recruiting the newest and hottest artists from every single genre who can bring the company revenue. A lot of these hot artists have been featured on publications, have a great turn out at their shows, or create a strong social media presence. Eventually, it gets to the ears of the A&R, and they are scouting the artist at their show. But, wait a minute. I'm still not telling you how to get a seat with them because that is what you care about. Hold on!

To get a conversation with the labels, (not through those dumb meet executive blah showcases), an artist must be a **NICHE ARTIST**! A niche artist is a small, yet upcoming artist who has the potential to be extremely profitable in the future. They have a specific market, but eventually that market becomes big, and so does the artist.

A niche artist contains or has the potential to do these following things:

- Sell tickets and merchandise
- Has a Unique sound or brand
    - Recall "Mirror, Mirror of an Artist" for this one
- Has some sort of team
- Is a topic of conversation in the music industry from social media to day to day press releases. This will be displayed in various forms of media outlets and through people.
- Has a strong fan base
- Attract people anywhere they perform even if the person has never heard their sound
- Surrounded by influential people in the industry that can move their brand*** Let's note that because this is hard.

I know this is what labels want from an artist because I was seeing it constantly in my 4 months in London. They don't want an artist who can't create the buzz for themselves! There are too many artists in the music industry from the self-releasing scene for these label representatives to give attention to all of you. In addition, there's just not enough time to look at everyone. If you can have all these features of a niche artist, I think you are ready to have a seat with an executive to get you a deal. Very impressive!

There is another way to infiltrate the label to get a deal, but I'm going to save that for Volume 2. What I can say for now is create that brand and network with everyone. Continue to make music and visuals that appeals to many. Become that niche artist that everyone will learn to love. Once you do this, there's no reason why you can't get a deal put right in your face by Nate Albert or any other A&R.

Consulted Projects

This part of the book gives you a sense of some of the projects I had a chance to consult with over the past year. I gave them some marketing strategies on rollout, suggestions on features, and also aided them reaching out to press. These guys have seen the success of Guided by Obas. I definitely think you should check out their work and let me know if you need assistance. These are their thoughts on their project.

Jxhar: *2 AM Fantasy*- 05/12/2018

"2 am Fantasy is about figuring out your place in life through the good, bad, and unexplainable." – Jxhar

Nazzy: *Autumn's Calling*- 08/23/2018

"Autumn's Calling was the first step of me growing. It signifies me letting go of all my demons up to that point in my life. Growth and change." – Nazzy

Meko Sky: *Thx 4 Listening*- 01/19/2019

"Thx 4 Listening is a state of mind expressing what happened after rising above the stereotypes placed upon us… the after effects aren't always good but Thanks for Listening."- Meko Sky

Maddadan: *Unknown EP*- 01/26/19

"Unknown is evolving as a musician and artist." – Maddadan

True Pax: *Midnight EP* - 01/31/2019

"Midnight is a project for one to feel in the soul. The songs are not depressing, but they are there for those who can relate as a minority. Relate to being broke, or someone trying to shut you down. Its an

EP that represents a good amount of emotion I felt in my life." –
True Pax

Inpaine: *Son of Douglas*- 03/12/ 2019

"It's the story I've always wanted to tell."- Inpaine

Apostle- *Kings Mafia* – 03/28/2019

"King's mafia is all about versatility, and to me, the project basically shows the inner cockiness of myself that i show once in a while as well as ending it off with real life issues."- Apostle

Nik Moody: "The Quiet Ones"- Coming Soon!

Conclusion

I know I just threw a ton of information at you, and you may be overwhelmed. I know!! The information I provided is all over the place kind of where my head is at always! You seen it in the **Guided by Obas Playlist** on Spotify (GO FOLLOW IT) and now, you see it in the book. This is how the music industry is. It is all over the place, but I hope I could provide you with the information needed to make it clearer. If you didn't understand the information, it's cool. We will be going further in depth with the Guided by Obas Podcast! This podcast is available on Spotify, Soundcloud, and iTunes Podcast. I will be talking about these topics with individuals from the music industry about their thoughts on these topics as well their journey in the music industry. You can stay connected with me on Facebook, Instagram, and Twitter to follow the journey. Let's stay in touch and keep working. Thank you for reading this, for you are definitely not late!

References/Links

Books:

Herstand, Ari. "How to Make It in the New Music Business: Practical Tips on Building a Loyal Following and Making a Living as a Musician." New York. Liveright Publishing Corporation. 2017

Passman, Donald. "All You Need to Know About the Music Business." New York. Simon & Schuster. 2015.

Podcasts:

DIY Podcast

The Questionable Behavior Podcast

Websites:

The Performance Effect

Helmon, Peter. "Watch Travis Scott Perform 'Goosebumps' 14 Times in a Row." Billboard Magazine. 17 May 2017. https://www.billboard.com/articles/columns/hip-hop/7800113/watch-travis-scott-perform-goosebumps-14-times-in-a-row

Moving Through Streaming Platforms

Spotify for Artists:

https://artists.spotify.com/

Merchbar: https://artists.spotify.com/blog/merchbar-to-power-artist-merch

Adding Tour dates on Spotify:
https://artists.spotify.com/faq/concerts#how-can-i-promote-my-concerts-on-spotify

RIAA Report

https://www.riaa.com/reports/2018-riaa-shipment-revenue-statistics-riaa/

Streaming Chart

Sanchez, Daniel. "What Streaming Music Services Pay (Updated for 2019)." Digital Music News. 25 December 2018.

https://www.digitalmusicnews.com/2018/12/25/streaming-music-services-pay-2019/

Tidal Rising:

http://tidal.com/#!/rising

The Crowd Goes "Fund"!

Setaro, Shawn. "How De La Soul Crowdfunded Their New Album With $600K From Kickstarter." Forbes. 30 August 2019

https://www.forbes.com/sites/shawnsetaro/2016/08/30/de-la-souls-kickstarter-success/1

Mama, "Can I be a Frank Ocean?"

Lynch, John. "The crafty way Frank Ocean got out of his record contract to release his acclaimed new album." Business Insider. 24 August 2016.

https://www.businessinsider.com/frank-ocean-left-def-jam-blonde-2016-8

Guided by Obas Spotlight Ursa Major:

Ursa Major: https://www.thelabelnoir.com/ursamajor

Becoming an Artist: The Artist Prelude

Seth Dollar, "Refs since Thursday":

https://itunes.apple.com/us/playlist/refs-since-thursday/pl.u-GgA5YpmupoDqDA

Where are those playlists?!

Indiemono: https://indiemono.com/

Playlist Pusher: https://playlistpush.com/

SoundPlate: https://soundplate.com/

Spotify Plugger: https://www.spotifyplugger.com/

Snap Me, Then I'm Gone

Salinas, Sara. "Instagram Stories has twice as many daily users as Snapchat's service — and it now has background music." CNBC. 28 June 2018

https://www.cnbc.com/2018/06/28/instagram-stories-daily-active-users-double-snapchats.html

Snapchat 10K: https://www.sec.gov/Archives/edgar/data/1564408/000156459018002721/snap-10k_20171231.htm

YouTube Links:

Rules to this Sh!t:
https://www.youtube.com/watch?v=cpUjBiB61gU

Joe Budden Podcast:
https://www.youtube.com/watch?v=CgXmkjjXkaM

NOTES

Thank you for reading. You can write your thoughts and ideas in this section of the book as well. As you reread this book, jot notes down and see where you need to improve. Just trying to help you!